# YES YOU CAN SERIES

# TRAVEL THE WAVES OF TIME - CONTACTING BENEFICIAL BEINGS

# MARIA D' ANDREA

# YES YOU CAN SERIES

## TRAVEL THE WAVES OF TIME
## CONTACTING BENEFICIAL BEINGS

By Maria D'Andrea, MsD, D.D., DRH

Inner Light/Global Communications

# YES YOU CAN SERIES

# Travel the Waves of Time – Contacting Beneficial Beings

## By Maria D'Andrea, MsD, D.D., DRH

© 2016 Maria D'Andrea

Published by Timothy Green Beckley

DBA Inner Light/Global Communications - All Rights Reserved

**Published in the United States of America**

Non-Fiction

Timothy Green Beckley: Editorial Director

Carol Ann Rodriguez: Publishers Assistant

Sean Casteel: Editor

William Kern: Associate Editor

Layout & Cover Graphics: Tim R. Swartz

Interior Art by Mark Taylor

Email: mrufo8@hotmail.com

www.ConspiracyJournal.Com

# CONTENTS

# DEDICATION

## To My Sons, Who Always Have My Back:

**Rick Holecek:** Who is analytical as well as intuitive, independent and enthusiastic about life.

**Rob D'Andrea:** Who is creative, as well as idealistic, independent and a visionary.

## FOREWORD

### By Rob D'Andrea

**YET** another great book by the author we all know and love. That goes especially for me, of course, because I am her son. However, that does not change the fact that Maria D'Andrea's books are excellent and extremely informative. Maria D'Andrea is a world-renowned psychic and author who has been deeply involved in this field for over 50 years. She was born in Budapest, Hungary, from a long line of psychics that have been doing this for many generations. Maria D'Andrea has discovered shortcuts and tips over the years to make practicing the occult and metaphysics quicker and more accurate. She loves to teach and pass along information to others, which is why we are granted the opportunity here to learn about time travel.

In this book, she teaches us the fundamentals of time travel. We will learn how to go on this adventure safely and also how to come back. This book could have easily been filled with mounds of boring data and technical terms, but instead it focuses on how to have fun and make the journey exciting. Instead of being extremely complex, she keeps it simple for us, so that we do not get lost or discouraged. You will walk away from this book with a general understanding of time travel and you will know if this is something that you would like to pursue further.

# THROUGH THE MISTS OF TIME

**TIME** itself is viewed in both esoteric and scientific terms. It is an illusionary period of measurement, formed by the brain to help us to function better in our physical realm. How else can your consciousness *try* to measure eternity? Of course, you can't. On the other hand, how would you, in this physical body, know when to meet someone at a specific location, when to go to work, when to do other mundane functions while on this earthly plane?

To give you a warning, we're about to get into easy, quick but scientific "stuff" . . . just for a short base of reference.

Time is a needed construct of outer awareness – generated by our mental perceptions – which moves within our consciousness. Our minds cannot easily accommodate the possibility of our reality being non-limited.

It is an illusion that is much needed for our day-to-day ability to function.

Time is a link, a thread, if you will, connecting all of us through energy as soul-minds in the universe. Maintained in the Akashic Records/Soul-Mind is all the information of our past, present and future, individually and globally, of all thoughts, feelings, experiences and events.

As psychics, mystics and shamans, among other masters, we can tune into these records and be able to "know" what the past, present and future hold. Knowing this, if something is coming up in the future that's positive, we should allow it to progress along its natural course.

However, if it is negative, we now have been forewarned so we can come up with a plan to avoid or at least improve the situation consciously.

You have to love the universe, right? Come on, you know you do . . .

Time is thought of in limited directions. It can also be looked upon sometimes as a time loop (situations that keep repeating) by some. However, mankind in general perceives it as going in only one direction – the sequencing of past to future through which we move. This illusion is

9

the most dominant one in our society. That doesn't make it correct, as we will demonstrate by working through the various concepts. This allows us to go back in time, to be in the present and to move forward in time as well as to travel to different dimensions and realms.

We are not limited by time and space. We are spirit living in a physical body. <u>We simply learn to ride the waves of time in our spirit bodies.</u>

Of course, there are several theories and treatises on the subject, not to mention the outlooks of Einstein, Kozyrev and Joy, among other brilliant minds.

Einstein theorized that space and time are not separate. They are a continuum and are thought of as comprising four dimensions. They are different aspects of the same thing.

H.A. Lorentz's model of time can be described as a double cone. One cone being on top of the other, with the top cone having its point facing downward and the bottom cone with its tip toward the top. This also represents four dimensional aspects.

We've heard about wormholes. This is one way we look at them to get a better idea: think of them with space being only two-dimensional, as a flat surface. The wormhole is a hole in the flat surface that goes into the third dimension as a tube and comes back out at the other end in two-dimensional, flat realities again. This is a shortcut version, of course. As are all the scientific concepts discussed in this chapter, since these are not the ways we will be working with time.

Taking the same scientific approach, "Star Gates" have already been utilized. There have been ways to build actual portals since ancient times, but you would need one of us as a guide to not be harmed and to go into the unknown safely.

\*\*\* We are going to shortcut, because although science is truly wonderful, *we* are not working in physical realities when we time travel. \*\*\*

Ancient people in various cultures believed that we are in a dream or in an illusion, so time is also an illusion. This concept is being researched by scientists as we speak. There are several names for this concept now. The Native American and shamanic cultures have been speaking of us all being able to journey to various places, all at the same time. <u>*I've named it - "Time Walking."*</u> The fabric of time is simultaneous in this concept. Think of yourself as standing in a spot having coffee, while in a different time-space you are, at the same time, walking in a park, then at the same time in a different time-space you are on vacation. And so it goes . . . Which one is the real you?

We are not going to go into all the aspects of time scientifically in this book. That would be a book all on its own. But we are going to be riding the waves with esoteric ancient knowledge.

Time travel comes down the line through shaman, magickal masters, light-workers, magi, mystics and various secret sects.

# Travel the Waves of Time — Contacting Beneficial Beings

We know time is a chemical reaction to thought. This covalent bonding is time density. We, after all, create our world, time, environment and lives through the power of thought. You will notice that wherever you put your focus/intent becomes what you create in your life. This can be good, bad or indifferent.

Notice, if you are focused on having a house in the next few years, you will eventually get it because your mind was focused and in "time" you will bring it to you.

You also have to take into account your personal time concepts. If you are having a wonderful experience and enjoying yourself, time seems to have moved too fast when you are done. It seems as though you just started having fun. If, on the other hand, you are at a job with negative, critical people, time will seem to drag on. The time was the same energetically and on the clock, but your perception was different.

Our brains perceive what they want to perceive. Some missionaries went to an Amazon village that had never seen outsiders. As the natives observed these visitors watching a film, they didn't understand because they'd never before seen any pictures. They had nothing to relate it to, so they didn't (see) perceive it. To them, the screen was blank.

Keep this concept in mind when we speak about intergalactic, super-intelligent, beneficial beings, beings from the past or future, UFOs, inner- and outer-world beings who time travel and that we seek to connect to/with. Just saying . . . it's a point of awareness. If you are reading my book, you know you're already open to working with a new realm.

As you can see, time has many factors and outlooks.

There are several magickal techniques offered in my book because a method that works for one person doesn't always work for another.

Remember, if you don't get the hang of it right away, don't give up. Didn't it take practice to drive a car?

We are working from multidimensional space/time formulae. We are not the prisoners of time; we are the *creators* of time.

# THE GODS OF TIME

**THERE** have always been Gods, Goddesses and varied beings that we can call upon to aid us in our quest to time travel. There are deities who can help us to learn more and to be able to "travel" safely.

Deities and other beings can be connected to more than one ability. However, here we are focused on the abilities that aid us in our quest for fourth-dimensional time.

You can also think of them as your travel guides . . . And you didn't even have to go to a travel agency. Well, maybe a galactic one?

A few of the beings we can call upon are <u>as follows:</u>

**Tiwaz** – Norse - God of the Sky

**Kronos** – Greek - Titan God of Time

**Arianrhod** – Celtic - Goddess who weaves cosmic time

**Isten** – Hungarian - Supreme God of All (which includes time)

**Time** – Angel of Time. It is said there are three angels: Time, Minutes and Seconds.

## YOUR FIRST LINE OF DEFENSE

Whenever you are working with other realms, it is imperative that you first do some form of protection to keep yourself safe from harm.

Even when you are dealing with a positive deity – and, of course, we only work with the positive – you are opening a portal to a different dimension. As this doorway opens, you might pick up "hitchhikers" that aren't so positive.

When dealing with the Gods/Goddesses and various deities of time, make sure you are safe. Use your own form or use mine and with command, respect and focus, <u>repeat three times:</u>

# Travel the Waves of Time — Contacting Beneficial Beings

"I am now protected by God (say whatever Source you resonate with), the all-powerful. I am willing to have (name of deity – if you do not have a name, then state the purpose) help me as long as it does not hurt my mind, body or spirit."

If you don't have a specific deity's name, you can say:

The Master of the Highest Order for time travel.

Always remember that protection is imperative to your well-being and to gaining the outcome your intent is focused on.

## SPACE-TIME/QUANTUM MECHANICS

Some scientists looked at space and time as two different things. Albert Einstein theorized that they are not separate but are combined into one continuum.

Quantum mechanics, very briefly, explains the paradox of the size of the atom.

You can look into the available scientific information to understand these concepts more; however, we are operating from a different mindset.

We are working with various realms to achieve our goals. Even though it is good to work with the scientific community (after all, the occult is the oldest science), there are several types of "work" that we do that are not understood by scientists.

So I say, we move on to OUR ESOTERIC WAYS and start traveling the universe and beyond.

## EXPECTING THE UNEXPECTED

**SO** here we are. According to much of society, we are expecting the impossible. Yet, since ancient times, in all cultures, information, formulae, recipes and stories have been passed down to us of all manner of otherworldly connections and communications.

We are modern day shaman/magicians/light workers/occultists, among other types of spiritual leaders. We use the ancient methods but we've also developed our own to be passed down to the next Initiates.

We will never know all there is to know. There aren't any limits to creation. We simply do our best to work with the energies that we have so far discovered.

Sometimes just changing our viewpoint will change what we are capable of achieving.

As an example, when you look back long ago, people thought only the Gods and deities could travel the sky. Then came the invention of the airplane, the rocket ship and travel to the moon. It came about because some people were not bound by thinking along only the usual lines of what is expected and what the limits are (unexpected).

We embrace the journey into the known and the unknown with equal expectations

What are your feelings when you go on a journey/vacation? You look forward to it and feel exhilarated. You expect it to be fun and to be a new experience. This is how you should feel when you decide to time travel.

What feeling do you have when you come "home"? You are coming back to your own body. You will feel a sense of rest and joy.

When I was younger and first experienced "travel," it was unforgettable. You will find it is very real and that you can recall it in detail, much as if you went on a physical vacation.

# Travel the Waves of Time — Contacting Beneficial Beings

As you time travel more, you will find yourself adapting to your new surroundings. I know in the beginning there can be a sense of fear and anxiety as well. This will subside, especially since we always use psychic protection so we know we are completely safe.

We are explorers who cross borders into a new dimension. We move in a space/time that is beyond the physical.

While we are created to live here in this world, we also live as spirit in our physical bodies and so are not limited by them. We can engage in discovering what is considered to be the unknown to many people.

You are consciously at a time of awakening to the inter-dimensional worlds around you. There is a book/movie called "Dune" which says at one point:

## The sleeper has awakened.

## Training to Travel:

As with any type of travel, you need to prepare. This holds for all etheric, intergalactic, inner-earth, inter-dimensional, and outer-realm travel.

## Physical training:

1 - Exercise is important in whatever form to keep you healthy and give you strength and focus.

2 - Physically pay attention to your spine being aligned (Ex: stand straight).

3 - Do abdominal breathing.

4 - Be aware of your body.

## Mental Training:

1 - Breathe in pure energy.

2 - Focus your mind at will. (Will power.)

3 - Focus on each of your senses, including psychic.

4 - Make suggestions to your subconscious of goals, etc.

5 - Focus on controlling your thoughts to being positive. When you think a negative thought, think of the word "cancel" and replace it with a positive thought.

6 - Practice visualizing.

7 - Thought control.

8 - Discipline.

## Psychic Training:

1 - ALWAYS use psychic self-defense.

2- Listen, pay attention to your intuition and move on it.

3 - Trust your insight.

4 - Self-knowledge.

5 - Use auto-suggestion to become better.

6 - Know Karma is real. What you put out – good, bad or indifferent – comes back to you.

7 - Have a belief system you truly are in tune with and fully trust in place. I believe in God, but as a shaman I look at it as there's One Source and whichever Path you choose to get there will work for you.

**\*\*\* KNOW THAT THIS IS ONLY A PARTIAL LIST. YOU NEED A "TEACHER" FOR HEAVIER OCCULT/PSYCHIC PRINCIPLES, KNOWLEDGE, CONTROL AND DISCLIPINES. \*\*\***

## TREASURES IN THE SKY

You can look at time travel as finding treasures in the sky. It gives you a picture in your mind that is not as limiting as most people's outlook. Of course, we don't really limit it to the sky since there are so many other realms to travel in.

I feel we/they are all expressions of the Infinite. **So, let's go visit the Light Bringers.**

# Travel the Waves of Time — Contacting Beneficial Beings

## Sky Travel:

1 - Protection first, protection, protection! In case I haven't mentioned it enough, right?

2 - Get in a comfortable position where you won't be disturbed.

3 - Take some deep breaths to relax and close your eyes.

4 - Focus all your energy on visualizing the sky. What color and shade is it? Does it have clouds? If so, are they puffy? And what color?

5 - If it is not calm, make it so it is.

6 - "See" a white puffy cloud hovering above you.

7 - Next, you notice that this cloud has an open door placed in its center. It is welcoming you to enter.

8 - "See" a rope made of white light descending through the doorway directly to you.

9 - You instinctively know that, when you put your hands around the rope, to hold onto it, and it will immediately pull you upward through the door at a comfortable speed.

10 - You also know that on the other side of the doorway is another dimension with positive, loving Light Beings. They are waiting for you to give you information.

11 - You are happily excited about this new adventure as you reach out and hold onto the rope and are instantly, comfortably pulled upward and through the doorway.

12 - You land on the other side of the doorway on the solid-feeling, puffy, white cloud. Allow the rope to drop by your feet. You see several beings of iridescent white light coming toward you. They are all very tall and slender and seem to be smiling at you in welcome.

13 - As they get comfortably close to you, they stop. They convey telepathically that they are time travelers and Light Bringers to all those who are ready to receive their help and information.

14 - You let them know that you are open to positive energies only and are ready to listen, see, feel and know. (You don't know in which form(s) you will receive the information.)

15 - Now, relax and just allow your mind to wander. Be aware of your thoughts and whatever else you may feel. Take your time.

16 - Don't try to force it, because it doesn't work that way. Think of yourself as a cup being filled up.

17 - When you have an intuitive urge to stop, then stop and thank them for communicating with you. Let them know you will come back to visit them again.

**Travel the Waves of Time — Contacting Beneficial Beings**

18 - Pick up the rope and allow it to gently lower you back down to your body. Let yourself float into your body.

19 - Take a deep breath and slowly open your eyes.

Remember, each time you visit will be different. Different times, places, situations.

# MEDITATION

**MEDITATION** is your way to tune into your Higher self and to connect to the unseen. You don't need to meditate to be able to time travel, but it does make it easier.

It is said that we should meditate every day and at sunrise and sunset. In our society, this isn't always feasible. If you are trying to meditate at the same time every day, but you have to be at a job or have something else you need to do at that time, it will only stress you out and you won't be able to meditate properly anyway. As long as you meditate when you can fit it in or when you feel the urge, it is better than not doing so.

If you don't meditate, you can relax by taking three slow, deep breaths. This will relax your muscles, which in turn relaxes you mentally.

If you would like to add a little extra to your meditation, you may add some of the following:

**Color** - Blue – somewhere on or near you. It is your link between the world of man and spirit.

**Incense** - Any incense you resonate to is good and they are *all* used for protection.

**Candle** - Best colors are: white, blue, purple, pink.

**Herbs** - Nutmeg, hyacinth, jasmine, frankincense, magnolia.

**Oils** - You can use the same ones as the herbs. You can also use cassia or sandalwood. Put a few drops on your third eye, heart and solar plexus.

## TRAVEL MEDITATION

Do your protection first.

# Travel the Waves of Time — Contacting Beneficial Beings

We are entering the realm of psychic energy. There are several brainwave levels. This is a basic/bottom-line explanation of them:

**Gamma brainwave** - This is your fight or flight level.

**Beta** - This is your everyday level, as when we are speaking to each other, working, etc. (To give you an idea scientifically, this brainwave vibrates at 14-21 CYCLES PER SECOND HTZ)

**Alpha** - This is your calm, intuitive, psychic-awareness level, where we will be functioning.

**Theta** - This is your deeper level of psychic/intuitive function and light sleep.

**Delta** - This is a very deep level where yogis can slow down their heartbeats, etc.

I would suggest that you read the meditation a few times so you can repeat it mentally with your eyes closed or record yourself reading it and play it back.

This is a time of activity (you are actively going into another state of consciousness) and rest (to be on a different, deeper, relaxed level).

**1** - Pick a destination to travel to. It can be anywhere, any time. You do not have any limitations.

**2** - Find a place where you can sit and not be bothered. Shut off all noise, such as phones.

**3** - Sit in a comfortable chair, preferably with arms, so you don't subconsciously worry about leaning over too much.

OPTION - If you are comfortable sitting in a yoga position, that is fine. That position keeps you upright and balanced.

**4** - Close your eyes and take three deep, slow breaths.

**5** - With each breath, count slowly backward from ten to one and allow your consciousness to become more and more open.

**6** - Each breath takes you into a deeper, more comfortable, relaxed state of mind. When you get to one, you will be fully relaxed and in an alpha state of mind.

**7** - Visualize yourself outside standing next to a tall, sturdy oak tree with its branches reaching toward the sky and its roots going deep into the earth. Notice that you are at the edge of an open meadow, with lush brilliant green grass growing everywhere.

**8** - You will now "see," a little to your left, a golden, gigantic open door frame standing by itself. It doesn't have a door, just the opening. Nor does it have anything it's attached to.

**9** - You realize it is a portal to a different time and realm. It is your doorway to your destination.

**10** - You walk excitedly and happily toward it.

**11** - As you get closer, you notice there's a mist within the portal. It is white light swirling and making you feel safe and welcome.

**12** - You don't see anything on the other side of the door. As you walk closer, you anticipate getting to the destination you have already chosen. You know that once you step through the portal, you will be exactly where you wished to be.

**13** - Standing in front of the portal, take a deep breath, feel the excitement and looking forward to being at your destination, then step through the portal.

**14** - Look around at your destination and take your time now to do whatever you feel . . . Knowing you can come back to this portal at any time.

**15** - Once you feel you are finished, come back to the portal, again take a deep breath and step through to be back in the meadow.

**16** - Walk back to the oak tree.

**17** - Know that you can come back to this portal at any time. You can pick various destinations and times at each meditation or go back to the same place.

**18** - Count now with each breath from one to ten, and with each breath you are coming closer and closer to your normal level of brainwave activity.

**19** - You are becoming more and more aware of your surroundings and the everyday sounds around you.

**20** - You feel happier and more energetic with each breath.

**21** - When you get to ten, slowly open your eyes.

You can utilize this technique, other ones in this book, or all of them. Remember that, at different times, we resonate with different techniques.

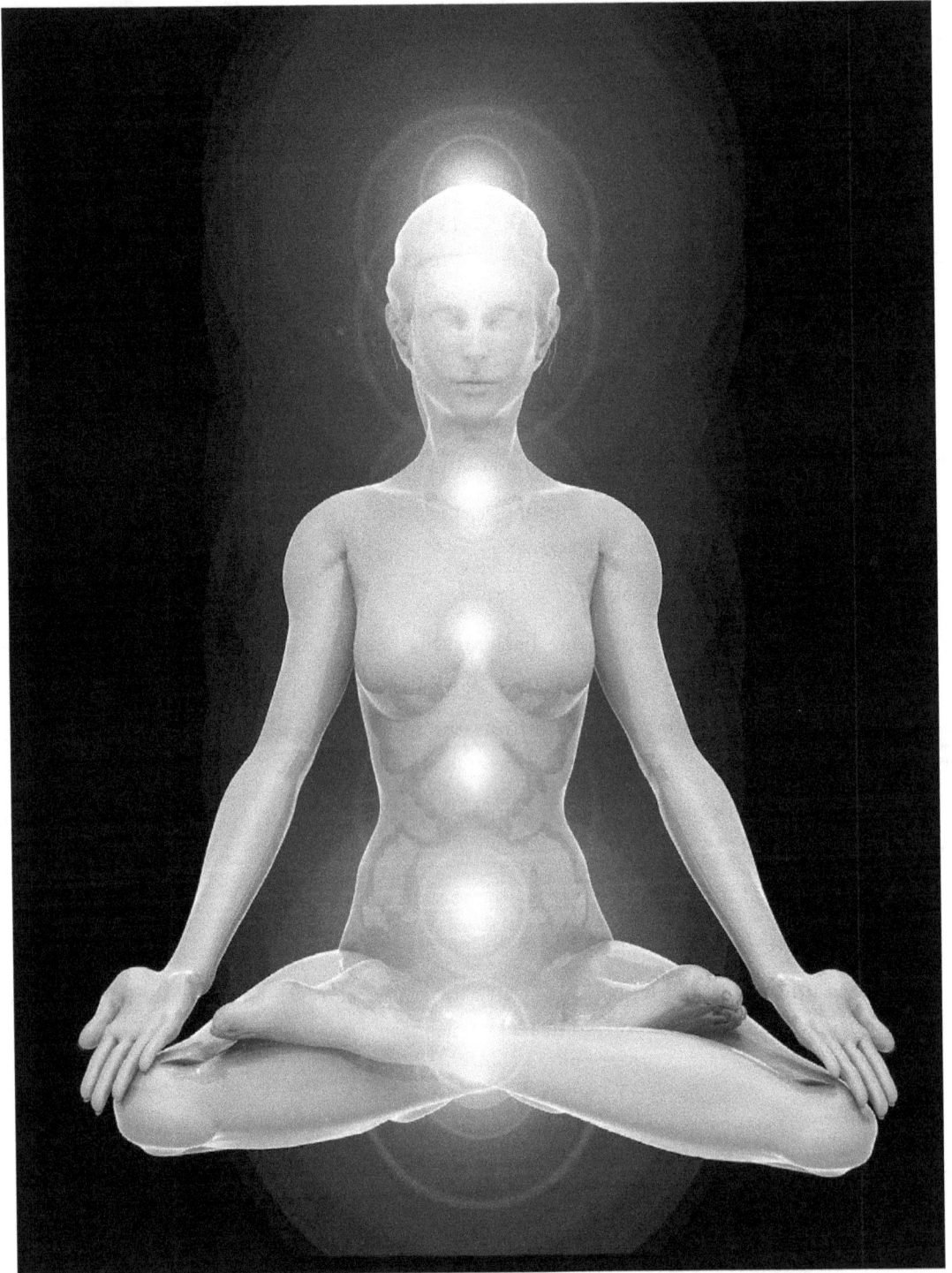

# TIME BENDER

This term refers to psychic experiences during sleep that connect to and show the person, while in their dream state, a locale in their past life or a future life.

This is a different form of time travel wherein you experience your real life path cutting though the limited, single direction/one step at a time approach to space-time.

You can tell it is not your typical dream. You can verify the authenticity of the scene by the dress, and it is easy to recall in the same detail every time you think of it. It is the same as when you recall a past event in your life.

We look at time-bending as we would any psychic situation where we go backward or forward in time.

This can also be called "retrogression" or "prophecy," depending on the direction you are psychically traveling in time.

We are still connected to our physical reality. So an alarm clock would jolt you awake with an uncomfortable physical feeling. Remember that when you do time-bending, you are safe. Don't misunderstand the alarm clock, as an example, as a negative situation. The point of this connection to both realities is the following: If there was a dangerous situation to you in your physical world, such as a fire, your survival instinct would immediately kick in and bring you out of time-bending.

The way you look at any *psychic information* is this:

> **1** - If you get positive information about a future event, leave things alone and just let your life progress.

> **2** - If you get negative information in your future, the point in knowing is so you can make a conscious decision to avoid, improve or fix it in some way.

> **3** - ***That is why you have free will.***

# Travel the Waves of Time — Contacting Beneficial Beings

In this situation, don't focus on a specific locale or time. Wherever you end up, that's where you end up. It's exciting to find out about your life. Now get excited. Are you excited? How about now? Come on, you know you're excited . . .

The following technique will help you to have control over time-bending:

1 - First, decide which direction you choose to travel toward. The past or the future?

2 - Before going to bed, get a full glass of water.

3 - When you're ready to go to sleep, hold the glass in your hand and focus on what your goal is. Are you focused on going forward or to the past to a scene in your life?

4 - Drink half the water while you keep your intent in mind. Then go to sleep.

5 - You will have your dream. Don't "push" for it. Relax so it can come to you. If you aren't relaxed as you drift off to sleep, it won't work the same way. You are creating delays.

6 - If you find yourself thinking of other things prior to sleep, don't worry about it. We are, after all, human. Simply go back to thinking of your intent. It doesn't have to be literally your last thought. Just make it your last *focused* point.

7 - The first thing you do upon awakening in the morning is to drink the other half of the water while keeping your intent for future time-bending.

Each time you do time-bending, you will become quicker at getting to your scene. You will know when you were truly at your locale because of the reality of it, as I said before. There isn't any mistaking it.

## Time-bending with a purpose:

There is also a technique branched out from this mode that can enable a person to do this for gaining psychic information for another. But you would have to have the control over this modality first.

## SHAMANIC UFO CONTACT

So, let's talk about UFOs. Are they real? Are they not real? I happen to think they are. After all, we can't be the only energy beings (yes, we are all energy beings) in the cosmos and universal realms. *Everything* is made up of energy. UFOs comprise one of our inter-dimensional connections.

There are several locations from which these UFOs originate, and you can easily read about various contacts in many, many books.

In fact, at a UFO convention several years ago there was a discussion about not calling them UFOs anymore since it could be said they aren't unidentified now and that we know a great deal about them. However, in many people's opinion, they aren't *all* identified and can potentially be from so many varied sources and realms that you can't completely change the name. They are still *Unidentified* Flying Objects.

This phenomenon connects to anything that is unidentified in the sky, whether it is felt, seen or heard.

There are known areas where these sightings are more frequent. The sightings in these areas are of unidentified and identified spacecraft and space objects that have landed. They are also areas where they have been felt, seen or heard on more than one occasion. They seem to occur commonly near caves with deposits of titanium, iron, other forms of metal as well as numerous other variables.

### The Story of the Chief:

I have a friend named Chief Wise Owl. In his area on the reservation, they are used to sightings of various UFOs. Of course, they don't think of them in those terms since these sightings are more common for them. The Chief said they've had visitations for generations back.

# Travel the Waves of Time — Contacting Beneficial Beings

Chief Wise Owl told me of one of the encounters he experienced. He said he was in a van with several other men from the reservation. As they were driving on the road toward home, they spotted a flying object. He immediately told them to pull over so he could walk over to the location where the saucer was landing and welcome the occupants properly.

The Chief said he became very upset because his comrades in the van wouldn't pull over and said they just wanted to go home. However, he would welcome the saucer people properly on their next visit.

It just goes to show you how differently people relate to UFOs and the beings in the crafts. *** You don't have to be in physical proximity to connect to other intelligences. You can connect from anywhere (your home, outdoors, etc.).

Even though some UFO sightings are in the physical realm, there are also unseen forces at work with these beings. We've all heard of how UFOs can be seen one moment and then disappear the next. They can travel between realms and we often don't see these other realms into which they move. It is said that the "ships" so far have been clocked at speeds of up to 18,000 miles per hour. Makes you think a little, right?

There is also an unseen realm where they never show up physically for us to see with our natural sight, but they can be "seen" at times with psychic vision.

Our involvement is not with the UFOs but with the beings controlling these "ships."

You may have a sense of time loss. This is not unusual. Time is a manmade concept and doesn't have the same substance in the other realms.

We are also traveling to meet with them. Not on the physical plane, but on the ethers and realms. These intelligences are recognized as having soul-minds and are living entities in whatever life-forms they take up residence. These are "other-plane" beings, space beings, inner-world beings, and some have been called angel beings and guardians. Through the control and use of different energy fields, some can take on human form in order for us to be able to relate to them more easily.

## THE BRIDGE OF TIME

LET'S go visiting . . .

Before you proceed, you should fast for one day (24 hours) prior to this ritual. You can drink water but nothing else. Make sure it is alright   with your doctor for you to do this if you don't normally fast.

# Travel the Waves of Time — Contacting Beneficial Beings

When working with stones of any type, first always cleanse them of any negative energy they may be holding.

One of the easiest methods is to put the stones into direct sunlight for three days before you utilize them. This could be any place outside or simply inside your house on your window sill, dresser, table, or wherever the sun will be directly on them.

For this type of travel, you will need the following stones:

## One of each -

       1- Herkimer Diamond

       2- Lapis Lazuli

       3 - Rhodonite

       4 - Jade

       5 - Citrine

Plus: You also need two pieces of copper. The size doesn't matter.

Body position: Lay down flat on your back in a comfortable position. You can lay on your bed or floor, as long as your spine is straight and aligned with your neck and head.

Your arms will be down at your sides with your palms facing the ceiling once you place the stones and copper in their correct position.

## Protection is a Must:

Put up protection. Yours or the following one, which is mine:

See yourself smiling and happy within two energy circles.

In the area that has # 1:

Visualize *Violet* Light energy surrounding you and permeating through you. This connects *Neptune and man*. This energy keeps your own negative thoughts and negativity out. (After all, we are human.) It will keep information that is coming to you clear.

In the area that has the # 2:

Visualize the color *silver* surrounding the violet. This connects you to the energy of the *moon*. This layer protects you from outside negativity.

In the area that has the # 3:

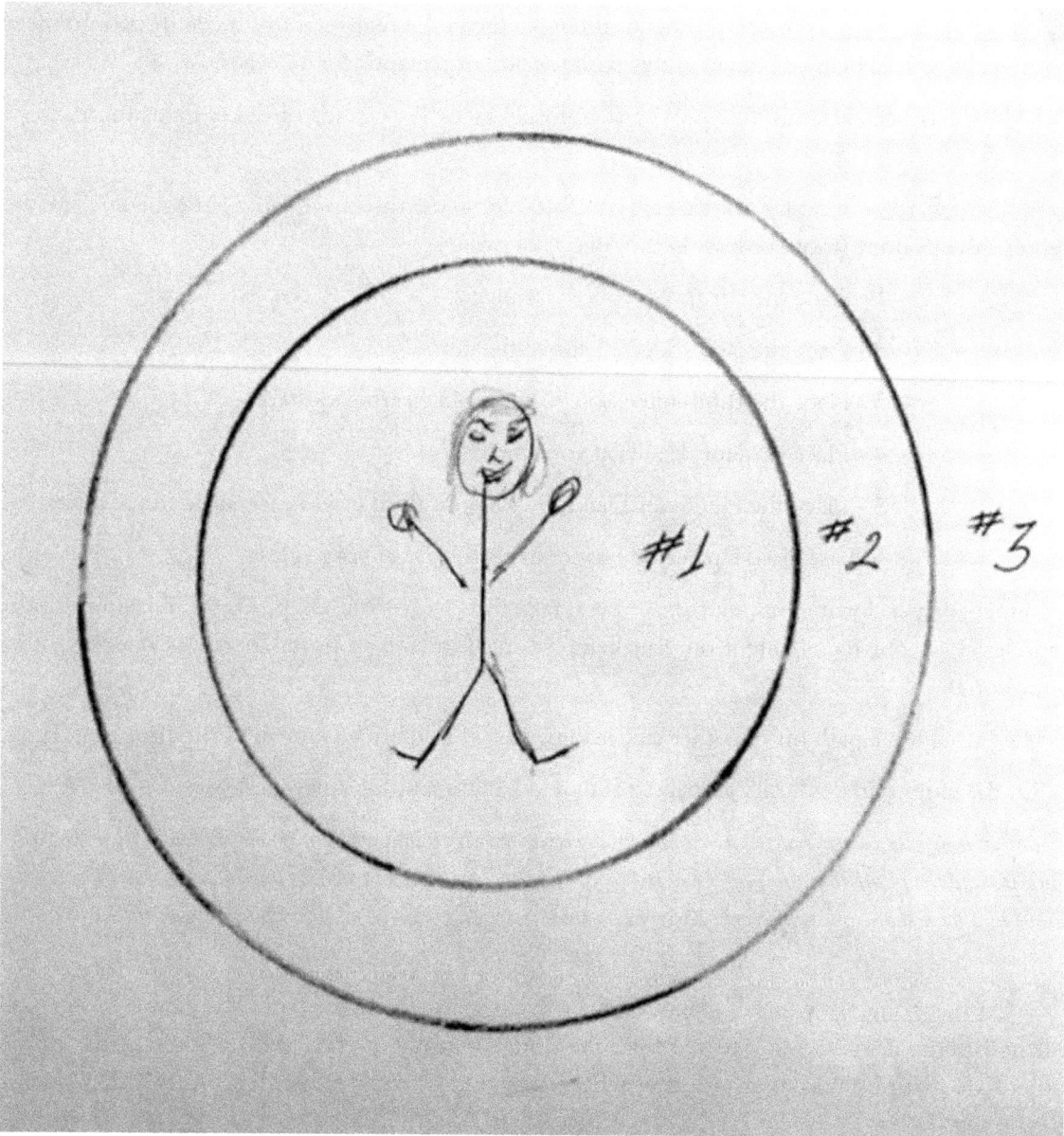

# Travel the Waves of Time — Contacting Beneficial Beings

Outside the two circles, visualize the color *gold* everywhere out toward the end of the universe. This connects to the *sun*. It forms a film that hardens your protective outer shell.

The next step - is to focus on your intent to travel the highways of time and space to meet positive, beneficial beings. Focus on this with joy and expectancy for 17 seconds.

*** It has been scientifically proven that it only takes 17 seconds of direct focus to manifest! ***

Afterwards - wearing something comfortable, place the stones in a straight line up the center of your body (more or less) in the following order:

**1** - Place the citrine on your solar plexus

**2** - Place the jade about 3" above the citrine

**3** - Place the rhodonite about where your heart is located

**4** - Place the lapis lazuli on your throat

**5** - Place the Herkimer Diamond on your third eye (on forehead in the center)

**6** -Last, hold a piece of copper in each hand at your sides

Immediately following this, close your eyes, take three very slow, deep breaths, relaxing all your muscles. Put your focus/intent on visualizing yourself opening a portal/doorway directly above your body.

The portal has a path on the other side leading to a sturdy bridge known as the Bridge of Time.

Put the vibration/the "call" verbally, with a loud, commanding voice, and state:

*I call on beneficial beings that resonate to positive energies only from all corners of the universe and from the past, present and the future that can help me to improve my knowledge on time traveling and to improve my life. Come to me in a form that is pleasing to see. Meet me on this Bridge of Time now until I send you back from whence you came. So It Is.*

At this point see yourself stepping through the portal onto the path. Walk on it to the base of the Bridge of Time. Look to see what the bridge is made of. You will see a mountain on the other side that obscures your vision of what is beyond. There is a light fog on the other side of the bridge.

As you step onto the bridge, you feel great and have a sensation of happy expectancy. Yay, this is a great adventure.

Go to the center of the bridge and stop. Look at the light fog and see who comes through. You will have a positive being meet you at the center.

# Travel the Waves of Time — Contacting Beneficial Beings

You may ask any question or have a discussion. The answer may come as a "telepathic" sentence or word; you may "hear" a voice; you may have a "sense" or "feeling" of the answer; or you may all of a sudden just "know." The point isn't how you get the connection but that you get one.

You can also ask who this being is, from where this being comes or any other questions you may have. You may get more than one being, but the situation is the same. They may come in their infinite varieties as beings of love.

Homeward bound. When you have a "feeling" or "urge" that says you are finished, thank the being for coming and say that you might call on it to meet you again at this same location.

Mentally think of sending loving energy to this special being.

Tell this being now: Go forth to whence you came.

Turn around on the Bridge of Time and come back to the portal. Then come back through the portal and settle back into your body. As soon as you think of your body, you will automatically go back into it.

Take three slow, deep breaths and slowly open your eyes. Take your time and gather the stones and copper. Stretch your body.

For future walks on the bridge, you may keep these stones together for travel to the Bridge of Time.

You never know who you will meet. It could be an intergalactic being or nature spirits from the past or future or even fairies (those elusive beings).

They like our company, and, as we learn about them, they are also learning about us.

What we do is serious, but we have a sense of humor. How can you not? Usually we have a warped sense, but then we do things others don't.

*** We are the explorers of time and space. ***


## SYMPATHETIC MAGICK

Sympathetic magick has been with us since ancient times and utilized by all cultures.

It is when you imitate a person, condition or event on a smaller scale to cause a parallel effect in the physical world. Science looks at it as cause and effect, the same as we look at it.

In this ritual you will also use the technique of sympathetic vibration.

# Travel the Waves of Time — Contacting Beneficial Beings

This entails a specific sound being repeated verbally and rhythmically. When you do so, it intensifies the vibration of the sound and brings about the event you are focused on manifesting.

A common example is when an army in perfect step marches over a bridge and it collapses. Another example is found in the Biblical story of the Wall of Jericho when the sound vibrations of the Israelites marching around the city while blowing trumpets brought the wall tumbling down.

## Bringing Down the Barriers of Time:

Remember to do your protection first.

Find a space, preferably outside, where nobody will bother you. If you can't find one, any room in your home that gives you privacy will do.

You will need white chalk that has never been used. Draw a circle going toward the right/clockwise until it meets where you started. You will be standing in the center of the circle. Leave enough room for you to be able to open your arms at shoulder height and still be within the circle.

You can stand in the center or sit (this is better, but a choice) in the center. Make sure you're comfortable.

Focus on your intent/goal at this time. Your intent is to travel through time to a specific place. It can be in the future, past or present. Your destination can be on this planet, in other worlds, the etheric plane or anywhere you decide. You are never limited. The only limits are set by you. What you think, you can achieve.

Mentally hold a picture of your destination while you chant. Keep your eyes closed.

## Verbally keep chanting repeatedly:

*Time and space*

*Do not delay*

*Open your doors*

*For me today.*

You may have a euphoric feeling after a while, dizziness or some other effect. Ignore this and keep chanting. Rhythmic repetition is important.

After a while you will "see," "feel," "hear" or just "know" you landed at your destination.

# Travel the Waves of Time — Contacting Beneficial Beings

When you are ready to come out of the travel, simply focus on your body in whatever position it is physically in and you will immediately realign with it.

Then take a few deep breaths and slowly open your eyes. If you are sitting, stand up (do not be in a rush to do so) and, going from right to left (counterclockwise), rub out the chalk marks. It is alright if you don't get all of it rubbed out. The point is to break the circle to reopen it.

## Note:

You will not always end up where your intent was to be. Time is a *tricky* thing. Where you end up is still valid.

## GOING DIRECT - ATLANTEAN/HUNGARIAN

**I** have had a friend/student for many years now. I am always saying I Go Direct. He called me up one day, and, while talking to me, he said  "IGD." (Representing - I Go Direct, because it's shorter.) Do you think I knew what he meant right away? No . . . but I should have. Life is funny.

In ancient times in several cultures, including Atlantis and Hungary (Magyar), the shaman had many responsibilities to the tribe/village that was their people. They were (and we still are) the healers, counselors, prophets/psychics, protectors, magi, spiritual leaders, decision makers and the connection to spirits in all their forms.

Spirits can be those who passed on, but they can also be beings on the etheric plane or multi-dimensional beings or nature spirits, fairies, elves, angels, deities. Well, you know what I mean.

These connections were also in the past timeframe or present or future. The information needed came from whatever source could help at the time.

You have seen pictures of a spiritual leader standing at the top of a mountain, looking skyward, with both their arms stretched out toward the sky.

Sometimes they would stand tall, sometimes they would kneel.

These leaders are not there only to go within themselves. They are there to communicate with otherworldly beings and times. The shaman knows how to send and receive information directly with these sources to help their communities.

They can commune with the "Gods of the Sky."

There are, of course, several techniques. We will be working from a very ancient one that is direct. Some people attribute this method to Atlantis, but it is a universal form.

39

# Travel the Waves of Time — Contacting Beneficial Beings

In fact, Native Americans, Hungarians (Magyar) and other cultures all have in common that they are comfortable communicating with other beings. This isn't something new.

There are cave drawings that depict someone standing or kneeling in the positions I shall explain a little later, looking at the sky. Many times there is a being in the sky in these drawings, which illustrates who the ancients were contacting.

Native Americans have said, as an example, that they've had spaceships land near their homes and they would have someone go out to greet them and talk to them. Then they would go back to their home and the ship would fly away to their home. This is still going on today.

It isn't only something that happened in ancient times, although, of course, not everyone doesn't discusses it publicly.

## The communication headband:

This is one form that's been utilized for communication since earlier times. If you look at pictures of shamans, spiritual leaders and other people communicating with what looks like nature, you will notice many are depicted with a headband around their head.

\*\*\* This is a communication device. Like the phone, it communicates in both directions. You will be heard telepathically through time and space and you will get information coming from there to you. \*\*\*

Make sure you stay focused on your intent while you work on the headband. Focus on this band being used for communicating directly with other intelligences and that you are not limited by time or space as you do so.

We are about to make this band with the following items:

**1** - Copper band about 1"-2" wide that can wrap around your head for the headband

**2** - A clear quartz crystal, terminated on both ends

**3** - Thin copper wire

**4** - Glue for the copper

You can get the copper and glue for it at a hardware store. Sometimes they will cut it for you to the length you need. You also may be able to get it at other places, such as a craft store. You can get a thin piece if you'd like to have it be more flexible. The thickness doesn't matter.

First, cleanse the crystal and copper by placing it into direct sunlight for three days. This is to get out all negative energy that it might hold.

# Travel the Waves of Time — Contacting Beneficial Beings

Take the copper band and, in the center, place the crystal with the points aiming toward the sky and the earth.

Glue the crystal to the band and then wrap some of the wire around it to hold it in place more securely. Don't make it too bulky because it will be uncomfortable to wear.

It doesn't have to be tight on your head. The band just has to be touching your forehead with the crystal in the center.

## Ritual:

When you are ready to communicate, go to the highest elevation near you. You will notice that many pictures depict someone standing on a mountain top. This is so you have the least amount of interference from society's energies.

If you aren't near that type of environment, it can be at the top (roof) of a building, such as in New York City.

The point is to get as high as possible, to get away from the hustle and bustle of society, as much as is realistically possible.

When you are there, first do some form of spiritual protection to make sure you are safe from negative influences and that any information you receive is "truth."

Next, place your communication headband on your head.

Stand with your feet about shoulder-width apart, your arms toward the sky, forming a "V."

Focus on contacting a beneficial being. You can mentally or verbally, as an example, <u>say:</u>

I call on any positive beneficial being to communicate with me through time and space to give me knowledge that would be helpful in my life. In return, I will try to answer questions that you may have to the best of my ability.

I open my heart and mind as long as it does not hurt my mind, body and soul.

Then be still and "listen." You may get information as a "vision," "hear" a voice in your head "clairaudiently," or just "know" or "feel" information. Different beings also communicate differently from each other. Just as people do.

Remember, it takes practice, so don't give up after the first try. If you don't get someone on the phone right away, does that mean you will never call again? Of course not.

# Travel the Waves of Time — Contacting Beneficial Beings

## SPIRIT HELPERS

There are those on the other side who have passed on who would like to be of assistance to us. There are also spirits that have never incarnated into our physical realm. Such as angels, fairies, elves, inter- galactic beings, nature spirits, and deities, among other realms of existence.

## Your Tools:

Mugwort - a handful of the herb

Clear quartz crystal

Two Tektite stones - small pieces are enough

A pouch/bag /handkerchief - best color is white, but any color

you're comfortable with will work

**1** - First, as always, do a form of spiritual protection.

**2** - Cleanse the stones by submerging them in water for three days to wash away any negative energy that may be attached to them.

**3** - Find a quiet spot and sit in a comfortable position.

**4** - Take the mugwort and place it in a bowl closely in front of you.

**5** - Place the clear quartz crystal next to the mugwort.

**6** - Hold the tektite, one in each hand.

**7** - Close your eyes.

**8** - Relax your body by breathing slowly at a comfortable pace. Focus your intent on a spot about three inches away from the middle of your forehead (Third Eye) and a little above your Third Eye.

**9** - Mentally say:

"I now open the doorway in space/time to positive beings only. My heart is protected; my physical body is protected; my mind is protected; my spirit and my soul are protected. I am safe."

**10** - Then keep "looking" (with eyes closed) until you see something. Sometimes, I find, it's like watching TV. Sometimes the sound is on, sometimes not. Sometimes it's in color as a scene, sometimes black and white. It doesn't matter either way because the point is to get the contact.

**11** - You will know when you are done because you will have the urge to stop.

**12** - Take another few slow breaths to realign and put the mugwort, crystal and tektite in your pouch/bag until the next time.

**13** - Get up and go back to your normal activities.

## LORDS OF TIME

There are beneficial/positive beings that I like to call the Keepers of Time. They are also called the Lords of Time.

They can be asked to answer questions about when a situation will occur or did occur. This doesn't mean they will always answer. There are situations we shouldn't know because we are not meant to change them in any way. So if you don't get your answer after asking three separate times then stop asking . . . after all, you know that you won't get an answer at this point.

This is not meant to be used frivolously. It is meant for serious questions. If you take it too lightly, they will not communicate with you. (Can't blame them, right?)

The Lords of Time are also aware that mankind is the only animal that has Time-Consciousness. We have an understanding of time in the past and future, not just at the moment.

We do, however, have what is called the "timeless-present." This is a situation where you are not aware of the past or future. You are only aware of the moment of "now" without any sense of time. This occurs, as an example, when someone is in a state of rapture or on an Alpha, Theta or Delta brainwave in a psychic state.

When they communicate, you can pick up the information in several ways. You might "hear" them speak to you or "see" what they want you to "see." Sometimes, you will just understand and "know" what the knowledge is that you have now acquired from them.

## How to Communicate:

We all work from time flow. This is considered the speed of thought. This unknown energy in the universe is a function we use consciously or subconsciously. It can help us to connect to the Lords of Time.

**1** - Use your psychic self-defense first. I know I keep repeating this, but it's very important and is always your base. Did you put up your defense yet? How about now? And now? Why not yet? Put it up. Go  ahead . . . (Sounds like the kids in a car who can't wait to get to a destination.)

**2** - Next, go to a place that's quiet where you will not be disturbed. Make sure if you are indoors that all noise is shut off, such as your phone.

# Travel the Waves of Time — Contacting Beneficial Beings

**3** - Lie down in a comfortable position. Have your spine erect and begin breathing deeply and evenly with your eyes closed. Continue to do this throughout this relaxation

**4** - Allow yourself to drift off.

**5** - Relax - Your toes

- Arches of feet
- Rising to ankles
- Upwardly to calves
- To knees
- To upper legs
- To thighs and hips
- To small of back
- Rising up the spine
- To neck and shoulders
- Moving downward to the upper arms to the forearms
- To wrists, hands and fingers
- Back up the arms to shoulders
- Then moving downward through the chest and stomach
- Again moving upward to the neck (making it loose and limp)
- Allowing that relaxation to move to the scalp
- Moving over forehead and brow (relaxing as it goes)
- Down to the eyes
- Now squeeze the eyes as hard as you can
- Now relax them and feel all the peacefulness and relaxing power flow over them
- Allow that relaxation to move to the cheeks and jaw
- Now allow a small space between your teeth so that your jaw can remain slack

**6** – Now I want you to visualize a bright luminous Blue Light surrounding your entire body (as though you are in a bubble of light).

**7** - See it protecting you, around you and through you for two minutes.

**8** - Right above your head, see a brilliant White globe of light.

# Travel the Waves of Time — Contacting Beneficial Beings

**9** - See a White ray of White light coming down into your Blue bubble. Think of it as a laser beam.

**10** - Next, see a ray of White light going from the White globe directly upward to the ethers and the universe.

**11** - See wonderful, positive beings made of White light who are the Lords of Time. Connect your light to them.

**12** - At this point, thank them for allowing the connection.

**13** - Speak to them with reverence, truth and love. Speak as if you were speaking to a good friend.

**14** - When you feel you are done, thank them and send them love energy as payment.

**15** - I want you now to gradually become aware of your surroundings. Sense the air you breathe, the touch of your back to whatever you lie on, the sounds around you, and slowly come back to awareness of your environment.

**16** - Then slowly open your eyes.

Remember, they do not communicate information to us that we shouldn't know at this time. You can always try the same question in a few months.

# THE LIGHT OF LIFE

## One of my Vision Quests with Time:

**THERE** is a Light that I saw in my vision quest many years ago which is difficult to explain.

There are things that we do our best to describe, but if you haven't been there yourself, we can only use limited language up to a point. As an example, there are exquisite colors that we simply don't have in this reality that we live in. How can we describe it? Sometimes people think we just don't want to give out some information, but it's that we don't know how. Many spiritual leaders often tell of these same intense feelings of universal love and other experiences but they can't really give you that same feeling or understanding that they have. You know, it's very frustrating to us.

As I was saying, I was traveling back through Time in a vast gray empty space. It was comfortable and I felt safe. I have been in this space before.

I remember how at peace I felt as I instinctively knew I was traveling into the past. I was not curious about where I was going or what was going on. I was just there for the "ride." I was enjoying the sensation of being free and not having any cares. I knew the time was so far in the past that I wouldn't have a year (#) for it.

Then, at a distance in front of me, I saw gray ledges. In the center I saw something that looked gray and plantlike. It had dark black roots that I knew ran throughout all the realms connecting them. Like a power line.

From the center at the top was a brilliant gold light that looked like a flame with a little shading of red toward the center. It seemed to illuminate all the realms.

I remember the thought that this was "The Spark." I wasn't sure what that meant, just that I "knew" it as a fact.

Then it went gray again and I was back after what seemed a short time. It was extremely vivid and I knew it was real. I can still see it today as if I just saw it. I immediately had an urge to do some automatic writing and drew a picture of it. Of course it doesn't come close to the experience and the detail and brightness.

# Travel the Waves of Time — Contacting Beneficial Beings

## YOUR TRIP TO YESTERYEAR

It doesn't matter if you are traveling in the present, future or past time. It is, after all, the same. However, we are now boarding the time stream for a trip to the past.

Do you have your travel plans ready to go? Are you mentally packed? Are you ready to go? Of course you are. Didn't you just buy the ticket to board? I'm sure I saw it in your etheric pocket.

## So, Here We Go:

**1** - Always do protection. (Have I said that before once?)

**2** - Relax somewhere comfortable, wearing loose clothing.

**3** - Pick a destination in the past. It could be in history or before that. You can pick a particular year as your destination point for now. You can also simply put the past as your destination, which is what I recommend to start with.

**4** - Close your eyes and slowly count backward with each slow breath from 3 to 1 three times: 3,3,3  2,2,2  1,1,1

**5** - Put your focus on the following: Visualize a comfortable, luxurious, beautiful, one-person boat floating in the stream of time, floating to you. Stopping in front of you.

**6** - Get into the boat and sit down in a comfortable seat. Or you can stand facing toward the front of the boat.

**7** - Focus on your boat going along this stream toward the past until you have the urge to stop.

**8** - At this point, the boat will automatically come to a halt. Look at your surroundings. You may decide to get out and look around or look around from the boat. Be aware of all the details surrounding you.

**9** - Speaking to the universe and the Lords of Time, ask questions, such as:

What year is this?

What realm?

If Earth, then what country? (If that applies.)

What culture are the people, if any?

51

# Travel the Waves of Time — Contacting Beneficial Beings

Any other questions you may have depending on what you see.

10 - When you feel you are done, thank the universe and the Time Lords for the help.

11 - Turn your boat around and come back at your own pace to where you started.

12 - Remember, you can always go back to various places.

13 - When you are ready, open your eyes.

The more "trips" you take, the better you become at it. Just like anything else.

## SPECIAL TOOLS

There are extra tools we can utilize for added impact.

When planning on going on your Time Travel, you can incorporate some or all of the following:

**Wear** - White.

**Monday** - Any day works, but this adds to ease of travel when you're new.

**Tektite** - Excellent for "travel." Hold it in your hand or place next to your skin elsewhere on your body.

**Clear Quartz Crystal** - Placed in room anywhere.

**Lapis Lazuli** - Place the stone over your Third Eye or near you.

**Amethyst** - Place in the room.

**Turquois** - Place anywhere near or wear this stone.

**Tiger Eye** - This is a protection stone. Place anywhere on or near you.

**Amber** - A fossilized tree resin, it can be worn or placed near you.

**Mugwort** - Place the herb near you where you can breathe in the aroma.

**Vervain** - Place close to you.

**Angelica** - Herb to be placed near.

**Comfrey** - Herb held in hands or worn.

**Peppermint Leaf** - Place near you.

**Bay Leaf** - Place on your body.

**Withes Grass** - Carry it.

# Travel the Waves of Time — Contacting Beneficial Beings

Eyebright - The herb or powder. Placed near you or on your body.

Oak - Any part of this tree can be used. Place near you.

Candles - White, silver, and/or purple.

Incense - Frankincense, Sandalwood, Rose and/or Cedar.

Oils - Acacia, Wisteria, Anise, Lilac and/or Cinnamon.

Copper - Place on your body or near you.

Silver - Place on your body or near you.

Sea Salt - Sprinkle in a circle around you toward the right till it meets where you started and is completely surrounding you, whether you are lying down or sitting up. When done, you can open the circle by rubbing part of the salt out of the circle.

Arcan - Call on this king of angels of the element of air.


By no means is this a full list, but it will get you started.

You can use the tools:

    **1** - On your altar.

    **2** - On your body – palm, heart, Third Eye and/or throat.

    **3** - In a ritual bath – add an oil, stone or herb.

    **4** - Oils can be used on your body, in ritual baths, and to dress candles or stones.

    **5** - Incense can be lit or a piece can be placed near you unlit.

    **6** – Near you.

    **7** – Any way you feel intuitively works.

Do NOT put music on during these journeys because they will ground you. You will not achieve the same quality with your experiences.

These tools help you gain contact, protection, harmony, balance and success. Think of them as an extra battery charger.

# ENCOUNTERS

**ENCOUNTERS** come in many forms. They can be on this plane of reality, such as with a friend, or in another reality with distinctly different, "other" life forms, beings of different dimensions and times.

Although there are negative and positive forces on the etheric planes, we protect ourselves physically, emotionally and psychically to avoid dangers and pitfalls in our adventurous journeys. The protection not only keeps us safe, but makes sure that we tune into only accurate, positive information.

There have been encounters throughout my life where I learned new perspectives, received insight, gained information for others, received and learned how to transmit different energies. I also had some that were merely extremely interesting.

## One of my Encounters

On one of my time travels, my destination was, as it sometimes still is: Wherever you take me in a positive, safe way.

After going into my protection and relaxation, I "knew" I had entered another dimension. I saw two beings who looked a lot like the statues at Easter Island.

I saw an electric green wire "outline" of two bodies. They looked stocky and serious. They were looking down on me as I was lying down.

The background behind them had brown "wires" – no apparent pattern that I could see.

I knew they were focused on working on healing me. It seemed as though it was for a long time and then I was back. I was feeling much better and more energetic.

I had the urge, as sometimes happens, to do automatic writing right after the journey. Those who know me know I don't draw, so keep that in mind . . . This is the drawing:

# Travel the Waves of Time — Contacting Beneficial Beings

## YOUR NEXT ENCOUNTERS

So let's get started on your next encounter.

## Journey to Adventure:

**1** - As usual, do your protection first.

**2** - Take slow breaths and with each breath relax, counting from 3 to 1, three times: 3,3,3 2,2,2 1,1,1

**3** - Allow yourself to feel all your muscles relax. When you have done the relaxation throughout your body, mentally scan your body for any tightness or unease. Command that part of your body to relax NOW.

**4** - Next, <u>say</u>: Divine Power, <u>(say whoever you consider your Source)</u> my destination is wherever you take me in a positive, safe way.

**5** - Allow yourself to relax and pay attention to anything you may "see," "hear" or "know."

**6** - When you have the urge to come back, do so.

**7** - Open your eyes slowly.


This doesn't seem like a long process, but it is very effective. The point is to relax, trust and enjoy the experience. You can add some of the "tools" I mentioned before such as a stone.


## SURPRISES

You will find that you don't always encounter beings or even something from your past or future.

There are so many situations that are truly surprises. We see colors that we cannot describe to those who haven't seen them; we see the steams of energies as they flow; the way the universe is layered in multilevel realms that overlap or are at a distance from one another, yet the energy lines connect them all.

We hear frequencies we will never hear on our home plane of existence. There are musical soundwaves of the planets, the sky and the leaves on our trees. The humming sounds of vibrational frequencies.

There are so many situations and amazing things out there/in there that I would love to show you.

# Travel the Waves of Time — Contacting Beneficial Beings

Practice, practice, practice, and you will open a portal to things you have never dreamt of.

Sometimes, when we see things, it is a short-seeming experience. Nonetheless an amazing one.

## One of My Shorter Travels:

I was traveling to another dimension. (You just know.)

I saw clear-looking, floating domes. They had flat surfaces as their floors.

They all looked alike, including being of the same size. There were so many of them.

They were electric blue on the outside and dark blue on the inside. Or at least those "types" of colors. That's as close as I can be in explaining the colors in a way that matches our reality. I couldn't see anything inside, but I "felt" these were homes.

I really wanted to get closer to the domes and look inside, but the more I tried, the more I knew I wasn't "moving" and getting closer. I also knew that, if I kept trying, I'd end up coming back, which is the normal reaction in these situations. But since nothing else was going on, I tried anyway. Those of you who know me already knew I was going to keep trying . . . right?

As soon as I pushed for that closer look, I was back. As though I didn't know that from past experiences. You can't blame a girl for trying.

Then I was back and doing my automatic writing. Remember, I can't draw even a dome. I'm lucky I can draw stick figures, but automatic writing gives it a different bend . . . (somewhat).

YOU can also have these experiences and many more. Who's a multi-dimensional being? You are. Persevere in your practice. Don't get lazy about it. You will find it so very worthwhile.

## <u>HOW TO GET HIGH</u>

**YOU** know I meant "Alpha High," right? It really is Alpha/Theta brainwave high. But I just shorten it. My students at my Institute – *"The D'Andrea Institute of Esoteric Studies"* – and private students are used to me. They will ask sometimes, just before I'm going to do some Readings, as an example: "Are you high?" Every now and then, I think someone will think we're going to have a drug bust. But we get high for free . . .

There are many different ways to achieve the Alpha High. See which ones might fit you.

Cultures down through the centuries have found ways to do this.

There are dervishes, yogis, religious rituals (such as breathing the incense).

We are going to look at some of the ways that you can choose from. Even though in ancient times they had some psychedelic experiences (mushrooms, etc.), it isn't legal in this country.

<u>Physical forms:</u>

<u>Martial arts</u> - Considered a moving meditation. I do Tai Chi Chuan and Qi Gong

<u>Sweat lodge</u>

<u>Floatation tanks</u>

<u>Tantric sex</u>

<u>Sports rush</u>

<u>Survival experience</u> - The high that you made it

<u>High altitude</u> - Mountain climbers

<u>Exercise</u> - Any form that gives you that rush when you're in the Zone

<u>Archery</u> - In Hungary, it is a form of the equivalent of Zen

<u>Spiritual forms:</u>

# Travel the Waves of Time — Contacting Beneficial Beings

Meditation - Closing your eyes and looking upward

Sound vibrations - Including: drumming, cymbals, bells, tuning forks

Fixed focus

Conscious breathing focus

Deep relaxation techniques

Biofeedback machine

Kundalini

Third Eye focus

 Candle flame focus - In the paranormal field, we look at this as it isn't meditation, but concentration (which we need).

Any of these techniques will help you to get a feel of what it's like to be on the psychic level. This will help you to be open to the realm of the unseen (non-physical vision).

Everyone is different. I find that when I'm working psychically or occult-wise for a long period of time, it takes me a little while to get grounded. Mainly because I've always been psychic. It's not a job as much as my way of life. I've realized that I can't get in a car and drive immediately because I will see someone that passed away on the road but can't tell how far ahead a car is that's in front of me.

However, both my sons are psychic and they don't have this bothersome side effect.

Some of us can feel when we're going through a "shift" in consciousness to move "up" a notch in our abilities. It can happen in a few months, a few years, once or never. It can just be that you didn't notice it at the time because it's progressive.

I find that when I "shift," I get headaches for a few days or weeks prior to the changes until I'm in sync with my new energies. I don't get headaches normally. A friend/colleague of mine says he gets a constant urge toward cookies till he acclimates. Go figure. I like his way better. Mine is just annoying at the time.

Some people don't get any side effects. Everyone is different.

Traveling through time, some people may get dizzy in the beginning; some might feel a rushing of wind; while others could "hear" some form of a sound. Some get blurry vision right before it happens or experience some other sign. Those might wear off through time or they may stay to let you know what is happening. Again, some practitioners don't get any side effects at all.

# Travel the Waves of Time — Contacting Beneficial Beings

## THE HIGHER YOU ARE . . .

After a time of shifting to a high, you will easily and automatically shift when you decide to.

It will be under your own control.

I truly feel that everyone is psychic/intuitive. My business, corporate and military clients like to call it a gut feeling. It is still a high . . . Maybe it's because you can't say you're high at work? Nevertheless, you still are. It isn't a visual thing, so, if you don't mention it, nobody can tell.

I feel it is a survival instinct. Have you ever walked down a street and felt that someone was behind you for a while, following you? And when you turned around, there actually was someone there? Of course, in New York City, it doesn't have much of a meaning usually, since so many people are heading in the same direction. But that feeling was your intuitive/survival instinct kicking in.

Everyone has this ability. Some people don't notice, some don't pay attention to it even when they are aware at times. And then there's us. That doesn't mean everyone should be working on it. It is not everyone's Path in this lifetime. It could be that they are working on other things, such as their intellect or material situations.

A person might come into this earthly plane to learn how to work with money. They might come in poor to learn how to work with this form of energy exchange and to do better managing their money. Or someone can be born into wealth to learn to help others. What they do in these situations is a matter of free will. The intuitive part might or might not be in the way.

## Getting There:

**1** - You know by now . . . protection first.

**2** - Take a day – preferably a few (seven would be great, as it's a spiritual vibration) to totally stop speaking.

**3** - That means that you may do this on a weekend, and, remember, you can't answer your phone – shut it off. No texting or email – that is you speaking. Don't cheat. You are only cancelling the benefits for yourself. Or go to a retreat or just away for at least the day.

**4** - You will be able to get your needs met. After all, if you were in a foreign country and didn't know the language, you'd still be able to eat.

**5** - It will be a little bit of a surprise how much you want to say to people.

**6** - You will discover how much you actually try to have control over others and situations. This doesn't mean it is negative; it is part of our everyday lives.

**7** - You will eventually realize how good it feels to let go, to know who you are and what your real goals are. You will notice things more, such as sounds like music and in nature. It is a time of reflection, even if that wasn't what you aimed for in the beginning.

**8** - Relax and breathe deep and slow. Or meditate. If you stare at something that interests you, such as a flower, and allow yourself that focus of going into the flower, you will automatically get high.

**9** - Take notes of your experiences.

**10** - After the initial shock of finding out how much you really control things in your environment, this feeling of surprise will wear off. You will find yourself more at ease, peaceful and in a better mood.

**11** - Think of people, as an example, who take a vow of silence for a while.

This will give you a sense of a high and how good it makes you feel. You might feel tuned into the cosmic energies around and inside of you.


**\*\*\* <u>NOTE: Defocus your physical vision</u>** – To be high and "see" the other side/realm, you need to be defocused in this reality. Did you ever see the pictures they make, where there is a picture hidden in the picture? To see the hidden picture, you stare at one point on the picture. Then the hidden one will pop out toward you so you can see it plainly. Same thing . . . Getting a picture like that is actually good practice.

Great, now I'm teaching you how to get high. Oh, oh.

# SECRETS AROUND US

LET us start with the government.

They are keeping so many truths hidden from us. We already know about time travel, aliens and experiments that various government agencies have been conducting and are currently working on. Why are such secrets necessary?

Some of my friends write about conspiracy theories, and it's amazing how any people are still surprised by this.

The government has been working with time travel. As an example, in October 1943, in Pennsylvania, they conducted what we now call the "Philadelphia Experiment." It was done by the U.S. Navy – "allegedly." Sometimes you just have to laugh.

It is said that the ship the USS Eldridge traveled through time and became invisible for a brief period. There were many complications from this and even injuries to some of the sailors who were present. You can look up more information about the experiment if you are interested.

There is so much that the government hides that it would take a separate book to even begin to catalog it all. However, we've traveled through time in our own ways and have had visitations from other worlds, so it isn't something "new" to us.

## Let's Discuss Secrets That are Positive:

On the occult/paranormal/metaphysical side, there is also knowledge we don't write about. After all, the word "occult" does mean hidden wisdom and hidden knowledge.

We do teach the hidden knowledge to students/initiates in private or in our groups and classes.

The reason we only teach it in this way is because – although we may kid around and have a sense of humor – what we do is serious. We are responsible as masters to protect people from

65

harm. If someone attempts a ritual, as an example, and they don't know everything they need to know, they can get seriously hurt.

As I always say: You don't see electricity, but you don't put your hand in the socket.

Music is a powerful vibrational force. The planets have their own vibrational sound, as do birds singing, wolves howling — all of nature has some form of it. Even when you are in stillness/soundless space, there is still a vibrational undercurrent.

Everything is energy. We are all moving at various rates of vibration. As an example, the earth's vibration is 1,000,000 vibrations per second. While a table looks solid and non-moving, think of all the molecules that it is made up of that are constantly in motion.

Music can alter your moods and thoughts. When you hear continual drumming, depending on it being a fast or slow rhythm, you will find yourself adjusting to that vibration. Fast tempos will have you feel more energy and provide the impetus to do something that takes action. Like dancing. If the tempo is slow, it will slow you down as well, which is good if you are relaxing.

Be conscious of your environment.

Colors also have impact. We all react subconsciously or consciously to colors. Black is a power color. Judges used to wear the black cloaks all the time. In business or in your life, knowing this can help you to deal better with situations where you have to show you're in charge.

However, you should be knowledgeable of where a person came from. Blue is a colder color to us. If you are from Norway, it is not.

We also work with various forms of light. One of the techniques we use that *you* can also do, goes like this:

Purpose: This is to help someone else feel better overall mentally and physically. Pick your target/person before you begin. Also, pick a time and day the target will receive this energy. As an example, you can do this technique at 3:00 P.M. and mentally program it so it is being received the next day at noon.

**1** - Need I say . . . Protection?

**2** - Close your eyes or leave them open, depending on which way works best for you.

**3** - Focus for one to three minutes on what day and time your target will receive this energy.

**4** - Visualize pure white light above your head.

**5** - See a brilliant white laser beam shooting out from it.

# Travel the Waves of Time — Contacting Beneficial Beings

**6** - Now, visualize this laser beam coming down through the top of your head (Crown Chakra).

**7** - Going into your head and focusing, it shoots out through your Third Eye all of a sudden as a brilliant white laser beam toward your target.

**8** - See this beam "hitting" your target and permeating through him/her and surrounding him/her.

**9** - Focus on this for as long as you "feel."

**10** - Then stop sending the energy.

**11** - Take a deep breath and slowly open your eyes, if they were closed.

The secrets are unlimited because we are explorers discovering new techniques daily while still working with the ancient methods/formulae/spells.

# CONCLUSION

**OUR** daily lives dictate which techniques/spells/formulae we utilize for various situations.

Time travel helps us to have more control over our lives, so our lives become more positive.

We learn about: who we are; the universe; the beneficial beings that help us in our quests; how we can become better as a person; how to help others; and what our personal and universal past, present and future hold.

Remember that attention and intention are different when you work with these energies. We work with *both* to achieve our goals. We focus our intention on a goal and our attention to send it out to the universal forces to manifest.

*Attention = attention is energy.*

*Intention = intention is information.*

Remember what mystics have always known: both matter and space owe their existence to the human consciousness.

Example: Fire-walking is an example of how consciousness affects our reality. If you think you can't, then you can't. If you think you can, you will be able to fire-walk.

You can reach the apex of your abilities. Nothing can limit you. After all, we are all seeds of the Divine.

You may decide to keep notes of your adventures. It helps you to know what formulae work better for you at various times. Notes also let you know how to improve the next time or what not to do. They are both important to know so you can do better and better.

There are always ways to gain the outcome that is your goal in a positive way. We always stay on the Light Path and remember Karmic Law and Karmic Justice.

Work with your intellect, intuition and also bring a touch of magick into your life.

Now go and pack your etheric bags for your next journey.

## YES YOU CAN!!!

# MARIA WOULD LIKE TO SPEAK PERSONALLY WITH YOU!

CONTACT MARIA D' ANDREA FOR. . .

**READINGS**
Private by Phone/Mail/In Person

\*

**WORKSHOPS**

\*

**SEMINARS**

\*

**BOOKS AND PRODUCTS**

\*

**MAIL ORDER COURSES**

Contact Maria D'Andrea at:

Mailing address:
PO BOX 52
Mineola, NY 11501
Offices on Long Island and Manhattan

Phone: (631) 559-1248

Email:  maria@mariadandrea.com

PayPal: mdandrea100@gmail.com